DOWN TO EARTH
Leader Guide

Down to Earth:
The Hopes & Fears of All the Years Are Met in Thee Tonight

Down to Earth
978-1-5018-2339-8
978-1-5018-2340-4 eBook
978-1-5018-2341-1 Large Print

Down to Earth: Devotions for the Season
978-1-5018-2344-2
978-1-5018-2345-9 eBook

Down to Earth: DVD
978-1-5018-2346-6

Down to Earth: Leader Guide
978-1-5018-2342-8
978-1-5018-2343-5 eBook

Down to Earth: Youth Study Book
978-1-5018-2352-7
978-1-5018-2353-4 eBook

Down to Earth: Children's Leader Guide
978-1-5018-2354-1

Also by Mike Slaughter

Change the World
Christmas Is Not Your Birthday
Dare to Dream
Hijacked
Momentum for Life
Money Matters
The Passionate Church
Real Followers
Renegade Gospel
shiny gods
Spiritual Entrepreneurs
The Christian Wallet
UnLearning Church
Upside Living in a Downside Economy

For more information, visit www.MikeSlaughter.com

Mike
Slaughter

The
Hopes & Fears
of All the Years

Down
TO
Earth

Are Met in
Thee
Tonight

With
Rachel Billups

Leader Guide
by Martha Bettis Gee

Abingdon Press / Nashville

DOWN TO EARTH
LEADER GUIDE

This book is printed on elemental chlorine-free paper.
978-1-5018-2342-8

16 17 18 19 20 21 22 23 24 25 — 10 9 8 7 6 5 4 3 2 1
MANUFACTURED IN THE UNITED STATES OF AMERICA

Contents

To the Leader

Welcome! In this study, you have the opportunity to help a group of learners as they engage in a study for the four weeks of Advent. Together they will consider an invitation to embrace more fully what it means to be followers of Jesus Christ, on whose coming we await and for whom we prepare in the weeks leading up to Christmas. The study's title, *Down to Earth*, is a play on words intended to draw us into a deeper understanding of why Jesus came down to earth. Participants will explore the implications of his coming for those who have answered God's call to be a part of the body of Christ in the world.

The Advent season, when we sense more palpably God's presence, is a time not only to pause with wonder and awe at the meaning of incarnation; it is a time to open our hearts and minds to how we can better reflect the light of the Spirit through a down-to-earth love, lifestyle, humility, and obedience.

Scripture tells us that where two or three are gathered together, we can be assured of the presence of the Holy Spirit, working in and through all those gathered. As you prepare to lead, pray for that presence and expect that you will experience it.

The study includes four sessions. It makes use of the following components:

- the book *Down to Earth*, by Mike Slaughter with Rachel Billups;
- the videos that accompany the study on DVD or via streaming;
- this Leader Guide.

Participants in the study will also need Bibles, as well as either a spiral-bound notebook for a journal or an electronic means of journaling, such as a tablet. If possible, notify potential group members in advance of the first session, and make arrangements for them to get copies of the book so they can read Chapter 1.

Because this is an Advent study, it is suggested that an Advent wreath be a part of the opening time of prayer. Advent wreaths usually have either four purple candles, or three purple candles and one pink candle. Check with your pastor to see if one or the other is traditionally used in your congregation. If a wreath is not available, simply place four candles in a circle. If regulations in your congregation prohibit the lighting of real candles, electronic candles are a good substitute.

Using This Guide With Your Group

Because no two groups are alike, this guide has been designed to give you flexibility and choice in tailoring the sessions for your group. The session format is listed below. You may choose any or all of the activities, adapting them as you wish to meet the schedule and needs of your particular group.

The leader guide offers a basic session plan designed to be completed in a session of about 45 minutes in length. In addition, you will find two or more additional activities that are optional. You may decide to add these activities or to substitute them for those suggested in the basic plan. Select ahead of time which activities the group will do, for how long, and in what order. Depending on which activities you select, there may be special preparation needed. The leader is alerted in the session plan when advance preparation is needed.

Session Format

Planning the Session

> Session Goals
> Biblical Foundation
> Special Preparation

Getting Started

> Opening Activity
> Opening Prayer

Learning Together

> Video and Discussion
> Bible Study and Discussion
> Book Study and Discussion
> More Activities (optional)

Wrapping Up

> Closing Activity
> Closing Prayer

Helpful Hints

Preparing for the Session

- Pray for the leading of the Holy Spirit as you prepare for the study. Pray for discernment for yourself and for each member of the study group.
- Before each session, familiarize yourself with the content. Read the book chapter again.
- Choose the session elements you will use during the group session, including the specific discussion questions you plan to cover. Be prepared, however, to adjust the session as group members interact and as questions arise. Prepare carefully, but allow space for the Holy Spirit to move in and through the group members and through you as facilitator.
- Prepare the room where the group will meet so that the space will enhance the learning process. Ideally, group members should be seated around a table or in a circle so that all can see each other. Movable chairs are best, because the group will sometimes be forming pairs or small groups for discussion. Plan for a separate table, or for space in the center of a table, for setting up the Advent wreath.
- Bring a supply of Bibles for those who forget to bring their own. You can find many translations of a particular passage at a website such as BibleGateway.com.
- Also bring writing paper and pens for those participants who do not bring a notebook or tablet or other means of journaling.
- For most sessions you will also need a chalkboard and chalk, a whiteboard and markers, or an easel with paper and markers.

- The writers of the study, Mike Slaughter and Rachel Billups, both serve Ginghamsburg Church in Tipp City, Ohio. They issue an invitation to learners to participate in a United Methodist initiative of sacrificial giving. At Ginghamsburg, the Christmas initiative is called "Christmas Is Not Your Birthday." Consult with your pastor or a representative of the mission committee to find out if your church is planning to participate in a Christmas initiative for refugees, for example, or if there are plans for another churchwide initiative in which learners can be a part.
- Because this Advent study will be taking place after many people are well into their Christmas shopping, consider suggesting that the group may want to schedule a one-session debrief in January just after the holidays, while their expenditures and holiday activities are still fresh in their minds, on the subject of holiday spending. Or the group may opt to have a session later in the year to consider holiday spending decisions for themselves, their families, and the church.

Shaping the Learning Environment

- Begin and end on time.
- Create a climate of openness, encouraging group members to participate as they feel comfortable.
- Remember that some people will jump right in with answers and comments, while others need time to process what is being discussed.
- If you notice that some group members seem never to be able to enter the conversation, ask them if they have thoughts to share. Give everyone a chance to talk, but

keep the conversation moving. Moderate to prevent a few individuals from doing all the talking.

- Communicate the importance of group discussions and group exercises.
- If no one answers at first during discussions, do not be afraid of silence. Count silently to ten, then say something such as, "Would anyone like to go first?" If no one responds, venture an answer yourself and ask for comments.
- Model openness as you share with the group. Group members will follow your example. If you limit your sharing to a surface level, others will follow suit.
- Encourage multiple answers or responses before moving on to another discussion topic.
- To help continue a discussion and give it greater depth, ask, "Why?" or "Why do you believe that?" or "Can you say more about that?"
- Affirm others' responses with comments such as "Great" or "Thanks" or "Good insight," especially if it's the first time someone has spoken during the group session.
- Monitor your own contributions. If you are doing most of the talking, back off so that you do not train the group to listen rather than speak up.
- Remember that you do not have all the answers. Your job is to keep the discussion going and encourage participation.

Managing the Session

- Honor the time schedule. If a session is running longer than expected, get consensus from the group before continuing beyond the agreed-upon ending time.
- Involve group members in various aspects of the group session, such as saying prayers or reading the Scripture.
- Note that the session guides sometimes call for breaking

into smaller groups or pairs. This gives everyone a chance to speak and participate fully. Mix up the groups; don't let the same people pair up for every activity.

- As always in discussions that may involve personal sharing, confidentiality is essential. Group members should never pass along stories that have been shared in the group. Remind the group members at each session: confidentiality is crucial to the success of this study.

1.

Down to Earth Love

Planning the Session

Session Goals

As a result of conversations and activities connected with this session, group members should begin to:

- examine their commitment to following Jesus together as the body of Christ;
- explore their identity as those who are called together to be followers of Christ;
- embrace what it means to be part of a down-to-earth people, living Jesus' down-to-earth kind of love.

Biblical Foundation

If you have any encouragement from being united with Christ, if any comfort from his love, if any common sharing in the Spirit, if any tenderness and compassion, then make my joy complete by being like-minded, having the same love, being one in spirit and of one mind. (Philippians 2:1-2)

Special Preparation

- If possible, obtain a plain red plastic drinking cup.
- On each of two large sheets of paper, print one of the following: "We have to agree" and "We have to win."
- Also obtain some writing paper and pens for those who do not bring journals.
- Plan to set up a simple Advent wreath, with four purple candles (or three purple and one pink, depending on your church's practice). The wreath can be as simple as four candles placed in a circle. Electronic candles are a safe and easy alternative to wax candles.
- In discussing a covenant of commitment, Rachel Billups lifts up the covenant of marriage. In your group you will likely have some members who, like the writer, are in committed marriages. But others may have experienced painful divorces or may be struggling with serious problems in their marriage. Be sensitive to those who may feel the burden of failure, despite having worked hard to make a marriage work.
- Read over the optional activities and decide which you might use. For the visualizing activity, you need access to the Internet, equipment for viewing a YouTube video, and drawing paper and crayons or colored markers. On YouTube you can find several versions of the song "Love Came Down at Christmas," including an animated version.

Select one vocal version and one animated version to show the group. At Wikipedia you can find Christina Rossetti's lyrics to the song. Print the lyrics on a large sheet of paper for the group to consider.

- If you decide to try using Mutual Invitation, give some thought to what issue might lend itself to discussion in a short time frame. If your church is conflicted about issues related to sexuality, it is probably best to save that discussion for a session when more time can be allocated for an in-depth conversation.

- If possible, borrow a chalice and plate from your church's communion ware, or bring your own goblet and a plate. Also plan to bring an uncut loaf of bread and grape juice.

Getting Started

Opening Activity

As group members arrive, welcome them to the study. If there is someone who did not bring a notebook or an electronic device such as a tablet or laptop for journaling, provide a notebook or paper and pen or pencil.

Gather together. If group members are not familiar with one another, provide nametags and allow a few moments for introductions. Invite group members to introduce themselves by responding to this prompt: "My name is _____, and my hope this year in Advent is…"

Invite the group to read silently the first paragraph of the study in which Rachel Billups, the writer, describes Thanksgiving gatherings in her family. She notes that her mother's pie serves as a unifying factor that transcends differing opinions and perspectives around the table. Ask group members to reflect on family gatherings they have experienced. Who was around that table? What was problematic or difficult in family discussions? Then ask a volunteer or two to briefly describe one family gathering. Ask:

- What issues tend to be contentious in conversations around your table?
- What (if anything!) functions as your family's secret weapon to unify the family at those times?

Tell the group that in this session they will explore ways in which the church can be a place where conflicts might be negotiated, including discussion of what factors might serve as unifying elements in the church.

Opening Prayer

Light one candle on the Advent wreath. Sit in silence for a few moments, then pray the following or a prayer of your choosing:

Come, Lord Jesus. As the light of a single Advent candle begins to illuminate the darkness, we enter this Advent season when we again await your coming. We yearn for a deeper understanding of what it means to follow you. Open our hearts, stir our will, and deepen our commitment to you and your community, the church. For it is in your holy name we pray. Amen.

Learning Together

Video and Discussion

Briefly introduce Rachel Billups, the writer of this session. Rachel is the Executive Pastor of Discipleship and part of the preaching team at the Ginghamsburg Church in Tipp City, Ohio. She teams with adult, student, and children's ministries to help make disciples of Jesus Christ for the transformation of the world. Previously Rachel, an ordained elder in The United Methodist Church, served as the lead pastor of Shiloh United Methodist, a multisite church in Cincinnati, Ohio.

Rachel Billups discusses the epidemic of division and disagreement in our culture, and the prescription that we are given during Advent: love.

- Share your response to Paul's challenge in Philippians 2. Has your faith made any difference in your life?
- During this busy time of year, what are some ways you remember to love?
- What do you think Jesus' perspective would be on the way we celebrate Christmas?
- What are some ways you use or could use prayer during Advent and Christmas?
- What are some ways you think God is calling you to action? What are some ways God is not calling you to action? How can you tell the difference?

Bible Study and Discussion

Though Philippians is not typically a book we consider during Advent, this letter of Paul to the Christians at Philippi is one of the most profound pictures of Jesus' down-to-earth love in Scripture. Paul was writing to these followers from prison, and the letter reveals that the Philippian Christians were experiencing dissension and divisions. Invite a volunteer to read aloud the passage in which we find this session's Scripture focus, Philippians 2:1-4. Discuss:

- Paul is posing a tough question: has following Jesus made a difference in your life? How would you respond to that question?

- Paul was not addressing an individual but the entire Christian community at Philippi. How do you think following Jesus might be different depending on whether you do it alone or do it as a community?

Book Study and Discussion

Explore Red Cup Issues

Display the red cup, and ask participants what it calls to mind. If no one remembers, remind them of the Starbucks red cup controversy of the 2015 Christmas season, and ask someone to summarize what happened (or do so yourself). If they have not already done so, ask the group to take a minute or two to read the information under the heading "Pies, Not Cups." Invite participants to call out, popcorn style, all the issues or areas of contention, whether trivial or more serious, that they can think of that divide Christians in the church (at any level from the local congregation to the denomination), and jot the issues down on a large sheet of paper. Allow a minute or two for participants to read over all the issues they named. Then ask them to rank these issues in their journals under two categories: minor and major. Discuss together some of the following:

- Which of these issues would you label as "red cup" issues— that is, minor issues? Why?
- Which issues would you label as major? Why?
- Is there any issue that you believe is important enough to justify breaking apart the church? Why do you think that particular issue is critical to the health of the body of Christ?
- What witness do you think our dissension on this issue is presenting to the world? How do these dividing walls affect how we treat one another within the body of Christ?

- Why do you think we often avoid discussing contentious issues in the church? What makes unity in love such hard work?
- Why do you think following Jesus is a "team sport"? Does that make it easier or harder?

Examine a New Way of Living

On a board or a large sheet of paper, print the words *Christmas is not your birthday*. Ask a volunteer to describe what the writer means by this statement. Then invite participants to take a few minutes to reflect on and note in their journals the answers to the following:

- What does my spending for gifts, entertainment, special holiday clothing, and decorations (either what I have already spent or what I plan to spend) have to say about the impact of materialism on the way I celebrate Christmas?
- Where does my life reflect an overemphasis on doing—on my achievements? As I evaluate what I am doing during this season, is it possible that I'm seeking to get a "gold star" from Jesus?

If group members are willing, invite one or two of them to describe one way they struggle with either materialism or their own self-importance. Then ask:

- What are some ways we can support each other this Advent season in turning our attention to Christ rather than to ourselves?

Encourage group members to reflect on how to focus Advent practices appropriately. Point out that it's not enough simply to curb our spending or do a few good deeds; Jesus' down-to-earth love is an invitation to live our lives in a new way, in a deeper and more intimate relationship with God.

Form two smaller groups. Point out the two prepared sheets of paper, one with the words "We have to agree" and the other with the words "We have to win." Give one sheet to each group. Ask the "agree" group to read the material in the text under the heading "An Invitation to Relationship." Ask the "win" group to read the material under the heading "A Covenant of Commitment." Invite the smaller groups to discuss their text and jot down relevant points on their sheet of paper, along with one or two questions. After allowing a few minutes for the smaller groups to work, ask each group to report to the large group what they discussed and the questions they raised. Invite the large group to respond to the following questions:

- What would this Advent look like if it were not focused on you and me?
- What would Advent look like if it were focused instead on Jesus and the kind of community Jesus is calling us to be?

Examine Active Love

Invite the group to read over the information about the parable of the good Samaritan under the heading "Do Love" as well as the examples from the ministry of Ginghamsburg Church regarding what Rachel Billups calls God's love on display. Rachel suggests that the first question we should ask ourselves this Advent is "How can I lend a helping hand?"

Invite group members to form pairs. Ask each pair to generate a list of ministries they know of in your congregation that represent lending a helping hand, as well as any individual initiatives of which they are aware, similar to the example of Doug Powell's "More Than Carpenters" ministry. In the large group, ask each pair to report their list. Then discuss some of the following:

- How do the individual and corporate ministries we named represent acts of compassion and mercy?
- Those who heard Jesus tell the parable of the good Samaritan would have recognized immediately that the one who showed compassion and mercy was not the person they would have expected, but rather the person feared and hated as the "other." In what ways do our ministries move beyond our comfort zones to minister with and for persons we may consider the "other"?
- What issues of justice contribute to the need for our ministries of compassion and mercy? What are some steps we are taking as a congregation or that we might take as individual Christians to begin addressing those issues?
- How are we extending, or how might we extend, these ministries to address needs beyond Advent?

More Activities (Optional)

Practice Mutual Invitation

Remind the group that Paul was addressing his letter to Christians in Philippi who had experienced dissension and disagreement that threatened to divide them. Similarly, members of the church today have differences that threaten the unity of the body of Christ. Invite the group to look over the list of issues they identified in the activity above. Together, choose one issue to discuss briefly—an issue of some importance to the group but about which there is also some disagreement. Try to choose an issue that lends itself to discussion in a short time frame. If your church is conflicted about issues related to sexuality, it is probably best to save that discussion for a session when more time can be allocated for an in-depth conversation.

Introduce the group to a process called Mutual Invitation, developed by Eric H. F. Law.[1] In this process, you as leader will *very briefly* share your views and feelings about the issue, but without projecting yourself as an expert. Then you will invite someone else to share. That person may choose to share and then invite another participant to speak, or the person may decide to pass, or pass for now, and invite someone else to speak. Continue the process until everyone in the group has had a chance to talk briefly, making sure to check back with those who passed or passed for now to allow them a chance to speak. A key part of the process is that during the initial round, no one is allowed to interrupt a speaker, even to ask a question; everyone just listens intently. After the group has had a chance to use the Mutual Invitation process, debrief together:

- How did it feel to use this process in discussing a contentious issue? Were you able to treat one another with love and respect in spite of your disagreement?
- Describe how it felt to listen without interrupting. Did you find yourself thinking ahead about how you might counter a point someone made, or were you able to focus on listening?
- How did you feel about those with whom you disagreed? Did listening intently without interrupting affect your sense of connection and respect for others? If so, how?

---

1   For more information on Mutual Invitation, see Eric H.F. Law, *The Wolf Shall Dwell with the Lamb; A Spirituality for Leadership in a Multicultural Community* (St. Louis: Chalice Press, 1993), Chapter 9 and Appendix A.

Visualize "Love Came Down at Christmas"

Ask the group to recall what they read under the book heading "A Covenant of Commitment." Particularly note that in the church, as in marriage, we agree to love one another despite our differing opinions. We also acknowledge that unity is hard work.

Call the group's attention to the posted lyrics of Christina Rossetti's "Love Came Down at Christmas," a poem that has been set to several melodies and sung as a Christmas carol. More recently, the Christian rock group Jars of Clay included it on a Christmas album. Invite the group to watch and listen as you show a YouTube video of the song (not the animated version). Then distribute the art materials and invite them to create visuals for the lyrics by drawing images, using words or phrases, or creating symbols. Encourage the group to keep in mind the true meaning and identity of the love that came down at Christmas.

After allowing some time for the group to work, invite volunteers to show their visuals and explain what they are trying to convey. Then show the second, animated video of the song. Discuss:

- What is unexpected in this portrayal of the song lyrics? What would you have added or taken away?

Wrapping Up

Ask the group to consider the examples given in the book of simple actions to lend a hand. Invite participants to reflect in the coming week on what skills and gifts they have, however small these may seem, that God might use to demonstrate Jesus' down-to-earth love.

Closing Activity

Encourage participants to read Chapter 2 of the study before the next session.

Remind the group that in the book, Rachel Billups describes a ministry called Open Table, in which she and her husband extend an open meal invitation to neighbors, church members, friends, and strangers across the spectrum of theological, social, and political viewpoints. She refers to it as a space for grace where people can wrestle with ideas. Display the chalice and bread next to the Advent candles, and remind participants that Christians come to the open table of the Lord's Supper, where all are welcome.

Recall for the group that the Lord's Supper is about remembering Jesus Christ and what he has done for us, communing together and celebrating. Invite participants to close their eyes and imagine that gathered around the table are people from all circumstances and walks of life. Ask the group to visualize this community as encompassing not just those with whom they normally participate together in the sacrament, but also those who may be strangers, who may hold beliefs with which they disagree, and those whom they may dismiss or even identify as enemies. Then say: "Around God's Open Table I see…" and invite participants to name aloud people whom they visualize as present and welcome at that table.

Closing Prayer

Ask the group to hold the image of the Open Table in their minds as you pray the following:

Come, Lord Jesus. Fill us with the radical love you brought down to earth. Open our hearts to you and to all those whom you love, friends and strangers alike. By your spirit, stir us to move beyond our comfortable places, that we may use our hearts and our hands to share your love with the world. For it is in your holy, loving name that we pray. Amen.

2.

Down to Earth Humility

Planning the Session

Session Goals

As a result of conversations and activities connected with this session, group members should begin to:

- try letting go of old attitudes and putting on the mind of Christ;
- explore their identity as those who are called together to be followers of Christ;
- embrace what it means to be part of a down-to-earth people, living Jesus' down-to-earth humility.

Biblical Foundation

In your relationships with one another, have the same mindset as Christ Jesus:

Who, being in very nature God,
>did not consider equality with God something to be
>used to his own advantage;
rather, he made himself nothing
>by taking the very nature of a servant,
>being made in human likeness.
And being found in appearance as a man,
>he humbled himself
>by becoming obedient to death—
>>even death on a cross!

(Philippians 2:5-8)

Special Preparation

- Once again plan to set up an Advent wreath, with four purple candles (or three purple and one pink, depending on your church's practice). The wreath can be as simple as four candles placed in a circle. Electronic candles are a safe and easy alternative to wax candles.
- On a large sheet of paper, sketch out five concentric circles, with the largest taking up most of the sheet. Label the innermost circle "Family"; the next one "Church"; the third circle "Workplace"; the fourth circle "Friends and Acquaintances"; and the outermost circle "Community."
- If you decide to use one or more of the optional activities, check to see what preparation is needed. For the dividing wall activity, you'll need large sheets of paper and colored markers or crayons. If you explore "Christmas is not your birthday," ask your pastor or someone who represents your mission or ministry committee to suggest two or

three mission projects that could be the recipients of funds this Christmas season. For the foot washing, you need a pitcher of water, a basin, and towels. If desired, prepare to show a YouTube video about the pope washing the feet of prisoners.

- On a large sheet of paper or a board, print the closing litany and post it.

Getting Started

Opening Activity

As group members come in, greet each one, with a special greeting for anyone not present in Session 1. When most have arrived, gather together. Remind participants that in Session 1 they explored the impact of our culture's materialism, which is fed by the frenzied spending of the season. They also examined their motives for engaging in the kinds of seasonal activities that might be viewed as working for a "gold star" from Jesus.

Invite the group to consider what old habits and ways of thinking they might need to let go of in order to experience Advent in a new way, more in line with our identity as members of the body of Christ. Ask them to respond to the following: "In Advent, I need to consider letting go of _____."

Tell the group that in this session, they will explore how to discover and live out a down-to-earth humility.

Opening Prayer

Light two candles on the Advent wreath. Sit in silence for a few moments, then pray the following, or a prayer of your choosing:

Come, Lord Jesus. As the light of two Advent candles illuminates the way to your coming, give us a clearer perception of your presence with us today. Help us to consider what it means to put on the mind of Christ. Open our hearts and minds to new attitudes and new ways of being. For it is in your holy name we pray. Amen.

Learning Together

Video and Discussion

Briefly introduce Mike Slaughter, the writer of this chapter and presenter of this video segment. Mike is in his fourth decade as lead pastor of Ginghamsburg Church in Tipp City, Ohio. His lifelong passion to reach the lost and set the oppressed free has made him a tireless and leading advocate for the children, women, and men who struggle in third-world nations such as Darfur, Sudan. Mike's call to afflict the comfortable and comfort the afflicted challenges Christians to wrestle with God and their God-destinies.

Mike Slaughter tells how God, the all-knowing creator of the universe, came down to earth as a baby at Christmas. God made himself nothing, and in this session we'll discuss an essential characteristic of the Christian faith: humility.

- What does it mean to you to say that Jesus was fully divine but also fully human?
- According to Mike, what was it that enabled Jesus to do the miraculous things he did? Do you also have access to it? If so, how does it work?
- Jesus taught us humility, but others teach us pride—in ourselves, in our school, in our country. Are these two qualities mutually exclusive? Why or why not"?
- What are some ways you check yourself regarding pride, in order to remain humble?

Bible Study and Discussion

Invite a volunteer to read aloud Philippians 2:3-8, in which today's focus Scripture is found. Recall for the group that in the first session, they learned that Paul was writing from prison to Christians in Philippi. His letter reveals that these followers were experiencing dissension and divisions. Discuss the following:

- Mike Slaughter states that our attitudes affect the outcomes of our lives, both in this world and the world to come. What does he mean, and how do you respond?
- What do you think it means to have the mind of Christ?

Book Study and Discussion

Explore Our Relationships

God is a God of relationships. Call the group's attention to the sheet of paper you posted showing concentric circles. Invite them to consider who occupies each circle of their relationships, beginning with their families, and record these names in their journals. In the innermost circle, for example, they might include the names of immediate family members, plus names of extended family members with whom they interact on a regular basis. For the other circles, they might just jot down categories of persons: their ages, gender, ethnicity, and so forth. In the final, largest circle, ask them to consider members of the community with whom they actually interact.

After allowing a few minutes for participants to work, discuss some of the following:

- Ginghamsburg Church has a diversity in ethnicity and political ideology. What diversity do you see in our congregation? How much do you interact with those in our community of faith who differ from you in some way—whether in age, gender, ethnicity, theological viewpoint, or some other way?

- What about the other circles of relationship we considered? Where in those circles do you interact with people whose life experiences or perspectives differ from yours? Are those interactions substantial and meaningful, or largely perfunctory?

- Having the mind of Christ allows us to see people as Jesus sees them. How do you think this might affect how we view and interact with people who are different from us?

Explore Humility

To know what God is like, we begin by looking at Jesus. Invite the group to scan the information under the heading "The Nature of God: Humility." Invite them to look for discussion of the following and what each has to tell us about humility:

1. God doesn't change, but the Incarnation demands that our understanding about God and people must change.
2. "We perceive that God is a god who fights our fights on our side, favors us over other people, preserves our way of living and supports our nationalistic interest."[2]
3. Jesus was not the Messiah people were expecting.
4. Jesus emptied himself of all powers and privileges of divinity.

Ask volunteers to expand briefly on the statements above, summarizing what the book has to say about what each one means.

2 Richard Rohr, *The Naked Now: Learning to See as the Mystics See* (New York: Crossroad Publishing, 2009), 90.

Examine the Sin of Pride

In order to embody Jesus' down-to-earth humility, we must deal with what is arguably the greatest sin: pride, which leads to every other vice. Discuss some of the following:

- In discussing the story of King Uzziah from the Old Testament, Mike Slaughter tells us that wealth and success should come with a warning label. Why? Do you agree? How is that demonstrated in the story of Uzziah?
- In the book, we are invited to consider the difference we could make if we refused to indulge in the negative mudslinging and political carping that are on full display in our elections. How do you think Christians might go about saying no to the current polarized political scene? What concrete steps might make a difference?
- In what ways do you think we as Christians live and speak what Gandhi called the "true message of Jesus"? Where do you think we fall short?
- Humility allows us to elevate our love of God and people over allegiance to religious, nationalistic, and political institutional traditions. What do you think it means to value people over partisanship, and how might we go about doing so?

Examine Dividing Walls and the Kingdom

In Philippians 2:7, the Greek word *doulos* literally means "slave," so that Jesus took on the role of slave in washing the feet of his disciples, thus demonstrating the upside-down, countercultural nature of the kingdom Jesus preached. Discuss:

- What does Mike mean when he asserts that it is doubtful whether Jesus' birth could have taken place in today's Bethlehem?

- What are some of the dividing walls of hostility in our culture that are in need of tearing down by Jesus' kingdom movement?
- In what ways is Pope Francis the antithesis of what people expect to see in the head of the Catholic Church? How does he represent an upside-down kingdom of God worldview?

More Activities (Optional)

Dismantle Dividing Walls

Revisit with the group Mike's description of the wall surrounding Bethlehem that segregates and isolates the Palestinian residents. In order to get an idea of the wall's size and appearance, invite participants with smartphones or other mobile devices to do a search for images showing the wall and mapping its location. (Images can be found by searching "Separation Wall" or "Separation Barrier.") Ask:

- What are some specific issues, problems, or areas of strong disagreement in our culture today?
- Like the Separation Wall, how do these issues serve as dividing walls of hostility?

Jot the responses down on a board or a large sheet of paper. Then form pairs, and assign one of the "dividing wall" topics to each pair. Give each pair a large sheet of paper and colored markers or crayons. Ask them to draw a wall (or simply draw a line down the center of the sheet to represent the wall). On the wall, ask them to print divisive elements of the issue. On each side of the wall, ask them to use simple figures, words or phrases to represent differing opinions of those divided by the issue. After allowing a few minutes for pairs to work, come together in the large group, where each pair can show their "wall" and explain what they are depicting. Then discuss:

- What role do you think self-righteousness and pride play in dividing people on these particular issues?
- How might we be called to build bridges over these issues that divide?
- Is there any issue or situation against which you believe you must take a stand (for example, racism) and about which you cannot compromise your views? If so, how do you demonstrate humility and the mind of Christ?

Encourage participants to consider how we can seek to exemplify the mind of Christ and demonstrate upside-down kingdom values where we disagree.

"Christmas Is Not Your Birthday"

In Chapter 2 of the book, Mike Slaughter tells us that since 2004, "Christmas is not your birthday" has been a mission emphasis of Ginghamsburg Church in which people at the church commit to spending half of their money budgeted for Christmas for themselves, then giving the other half to a cause that honors Jesus' birth. If you generated a list of ministries in your church that represent offering a helping hand, revisit the list. Also give the group some information about ministry or mission projects suggested by your pastor or a member of a mission or ministry committee.

Acknowledge that by this time in Advent many people are well into Christmas shopping, if not finished. But suggest that it is still possible to consider allocating some of the budgeted gift money for one of these causes that honors Jesus' birthday. Invite the group to brainstorm ways to take small steps toward a fuller commitment next Christmas, such as placing a bank on the dining room table to collect change for a particular project all during the coming year.

Participate in a Foot Washing

Ask a volunteer to summarize the anecdote about Pope Francis given at the beginning of Chapter 2. Point out that in 2014, the pope defied tradition again, this time by washing the feet of people who were elderly and living with a disability. If desired, watch a YouTube clip about the controversy surrounding the pope's unorthodox actions. Discuss:

- How did the pope's actions show humility?
- What was controversial about how he went about washing feet and whose feet he washed?

Note that though this practice is traditionally done on Maundy Thursday, it can be a symbol of humility during Advent. Invite the group to form a circle, and encourage those who want to have their feet washed to remove their shoes and socks. Pour some water from the pitcher into the basin. Stress that if anyone feels uncomfortable, they can offer their hands instead, or simply indicate they would like to pass. Group members can begin by washing the feet or hands of the person to their right, then passing the basin and towels to that person, who washes the feet or hands of the person to *their* right. Continue around the circle until all who desire to participate have had the opportunity. Discuss:

- How did Jesus demonstrate humility by washing the feet of his disciples?
- What was the experience of washing someone else's feet like for you? How did it feel to have your own feet washed? What are comparable practices in our culture that might serve to exemplify humility?

Wrapping Up

Remind participants to read Chapter 3 before the next session.

Invite the group to consider again the opening activity in which they responded to the following prompt: "In Advent, I need to consider letting go of _____." Encourage them to jot this prompt down in their journals and to reflect on it in the coming week.

Ask them then to reflect on the following: "In Advent, I need to consider new attitudes in line with the mind of Christ." In the course of the week as they go about their normal seasonal routines, encourage group members to give thought to how down-to-earth humility might transform their interactions with others.

Closing Activity

In exploring what ultimately determines the authenticity of our faith, we should remember that it's not the validity of our theological positions. Rather, it's in demonstrating Christlike love. Ask the group to listen as a volunteer reads aloud 1 Corinthians 13.

Invite the group to reflect on the upside-down, countercultural nature of God's kingdom as they join together in this litany from the Sermon on the Mount (Matthew 5), Jesus' teaching about Judgment Day (Matthew 25), and Paul's words in Galatians 3, displayed on the paper you prepared before the session:

Leader: To be blessed,
All: you must bless others.

Leader: To be forgiven,
All: you have to forgive others.

Leader: To not be judged,
All: you must not judge others.

Leader: The first will be last
All: **and the last first.**

Leader: You must lose yourself
All: **to find yourself.**

Leader: You must first give
All: **before you can receive.**

Leader: The poor inherit the kingdom of Heaven.
All: **The meek will inherit the earth.**

Leader: Peacemakers will be called children of God.
All: **There is neither Jew nor Gentile, neither slave nor free, neither male nor female, for all are one in Christ.**

Leader: The hungry are fed.
All: **Safe water is provided for the thirsty.**

Leader: The sick are ministered to.
All: **The prisoners are visited.**

Leader: The refugee is provided shelter.
All: **The poor are clothed.**

Closing Prayer

Come, Lord Jesus. By your spirit, guide us in letting go of pride and embracing your down-to-earth humility. Open our minds to your mind, that we may reflect your love more fully. For in your holy name, the one born in a humble stable, we pray. Amen.

3.

Down to Earth Lifestyle

Planning the Session

Session Goals

As a result of conversations and activities connected with this session, group members should begin to:

- examine how God's Spirit equips us to live a faith-based lifestyle;
- explore our identity as those who are called together to be followers of Christ;
- embrace what it means to be part of a down-to-earth people, living Jesus' down-to-earth lifestyle.

Biblical Foundation

When Joseph woke up, he did what the angel of the Lord commanded him and took Mary home as his wife. (Matthew 1:24)

Special Preparation

- Again set up a simple Advent wreath, with four purple candles, or simply place four candles in a circle. Electronic candles are a safe and easy alternative to wax candles. If you are using a pink candle, the third Sunday in Advent is traditionally the day the pink candle is lit.
- If you decide to do one or more of the optional activities, check to see what preparation is needed. For the activity on exploring hope for Syrian refugees, you will need Internet access if you would like to show the video, "Beyond Bethlehem: Christmas Hope for Refugees" (at http://www.ginghamsburg.org/miracleoffering), as well as equipment for viewing the video. Also alert your pastor or a representative of your mission committee that you will be discussing involvement in this mission initiative. If your church has already made a commitment to participate in this campaign, you will want to partner with those already working on the initiative.
- For the optional activity on exploring visions, you will need three or four large sheets of paper and colored markers. On each sheet, print the following, with space to respond: "For this issue, my dream is...My vision for responding to this issue is..."
- For the optional activity on towel carriers, get some heavyweight paper towels (or gather some white copy paper) and fine-lined felt-tipped markers.

Getting Started

Opening Activity

Welcome participants as they arrive, with a special welcome for newcomers. When most group members have arrived, gather together. Invite group members to revisit the statement they were to reflect on following last session: "In Advent, I need to consider new attitudes in line with the mind of Christ."

Invite volunteers to report whether focusing on down-to-earth humility since the last session changed their interactions with others in any way. Did they find their normal holiday routines altered in some way? Were they more mindful of activities in which they chose to engage?

Encourage participants to think about any dreams they remember. Ask:

- Have you ever had a dream that, upon your waking, seemed to have a message for you? If so, describe the dream. What actions, if any, did you take in response to the dream?
- Do you believe God can speak to people through dreams? Why or why not?

Tell the group that in this session, we are invited to explore what Mike Slaughter calls "God dreams" and the relationship between God dreams and living a down-to-earth lifestyle.

Opening Prayer

Light three candles on the Advent wreath. Sit in silence for a few moments, then pray the following, or a prayer of your choosing:

Come, Lord Jesus. As the light of three Advent candles illuminates the way to your coming, open our hearts and minds to the light of

41

new visions, that we may be empowered to live more fully as your
followers. For we pray in your holy name. Amen.

Learning Together

Video and Discussion

Mike Slaughter tells us that the invitation of Jesus is costly. Jesus said, "Whoever wants to be my disciple must take up their cross daily and follow me." In this session we'll discuss what it takes to live a down-to-earth lifestyle.

- Mike says that Jesus revealed a God of "downward mobility." What do you think he means, and how might it apply to our own lives?
- The kingdom Jesus described was "upside down." What does this mean, and what are some examples of it?
- Mike says God is all about the common good. What does that mean for us today in a world that's divided?

Bible Study and Discussion

Ask the group to listen as a volunteer reads aloud Matthew 1:18-25, in which today's focus Scripture is found. Invite participants to review quickly the information at the beginning of Chapter 3 about marriage and betrothal practices in the first century. Discuss:

- Imagine yourself to be in Joseph's shoes. What emotions do you think you would have been experiencing after waking from this unusual dream? How do you think you might have responded?
- It's tempting to spiritualize the events of the Christmas story, ignoring the down-to-earth realities of everyday life at the time. In practical terms, what do you imagine the cost was to Joseph of acting as he did?

Book Study and Discussion
Explore God Dreams and Faith

The ability to experience God dreams makes real the Holy Spirit's presence with us and in us, and the Spirit resources us to live faith-based lifestyles and to participate as God's partners in mission. Discuss:

- Mike Slaughter observes that faith is perhaps the most underutilized asset in the church. How do you respond?
- In discussing Jesus' encounter with the man at the Bethesda healing pool, Mike states that it's easy to hold to a form of faith and still deny faith's power. What does he mean by this statement, and how do you respond?
- What are the two components of every miracle, as described by Mike? He observes that making faith commitments on a daily basis has exponential results. What do you think? Have you experienced such results in your own faith life?

Explore Ministries of Carrying the Towel

Remind the group that in book Chapter 2, they read about the actions of Pope Francis when he washed the feet of prisoners in a youth prison on Maundy Thursday. This act of humility generated controversy among some traditional Catholics, who were shocked at the act of washing prisoners' feet and especially the feet of women, rather than washing the feet of priests as had been the practice of previous popes during Holy Week.

Chapter 3 includes an examination of the servant lifestyle as exemplified in Jesus' washing of the disciples' feet. If your group engaged in foot washing in the previous session (one of the optional activities), or if group members have participated in foot washing at some other time, ask them to describe how they responded to washing feet and to having their own feet washed.

Invite the group to review the information under the heading, "The God of the Towel." Discuss some of the following together:

- What would have been so shocking to the disciples about having Jesus wash their feet?
- What is the significance of the order of wording (*Teacher* and *Lord*) and how Jesus changes it to make a point?
- Mike Slaughter observes that faith can never be separated from a lifestyle of compassionate action. What does this have to say about one's lifestyle as a follower of Christ? In your own faith life, where do you experience this connection?

Invite two volunteers to summarize the stories of Dorothy Stang and the Garrett family, two examples of people who "carry the towel." Discuss:

- How did each of these people demonstrate obedience to Christ's call? What sacrifices did each make on behalf of God's kingdom?

Not every Christian is called to make sacrifices at the level of those made by Dorothy Stang and the Garrett family. Even so, the Christian lifestyle does come with inherent risks. Invite participants to reflect on the following question to ponder in their journals:

- Where in my own faith life do I feel called to embrace a lifestyle of sacrificial love?

Suggest that some in the group may not yet have sensed God calling them to particular actions that reflect sacrificial love, but that an attitude of intentional openness to that call may allow them to be more attentive to the working of the Spirit. Encourage them to make petitions for discernment about what God is calling them to do and be a part of their prayer life.

Call the group's attention to what Mike Slaughter has to say in Chapter 3 about greatness, and invite the group to give examples from the story of Jesus' birth about how his coming turned ideas of power and greatness upside down. Discuss some of the following:

- Jesus demonstrated that leadership means being elevated in influence by being lowered to the place of greatest need. Mike asserts that increased responsibility will always mean decreased privilege. What does he mean, and how do you respond? Do you think it is easy to voluntarily set aside privilege? Why or why not?
- How is leadership defined in our culture? How would you say this definition of leadership differs from our cultural understandings of who a leader is?
- Mike cites his colleague Rachel Billups as an example of one who demonstrates true servant leadership. Who are some servant leaders you can name? How do they demonstrate the quality of leadership?

More Activities (Optional)

Explore Hope for Syrian Refugees

Ask the group to review the information under the heading "A Down-to-Earth Vision" about the role of Ginghamsburg Church in partnering with the United Methodist Committee on Relief (UMCOR) to address the Syrian refugee crisis. Show the video clip, "Beyond Bethlehem: Christmas Hope for Refugees," described in the section above called Special Preparation. Invite the group to discuss what they saw:

- What was surprising or was new information for you?
- What aspects of the video were most powerful for you? Why?

On a large sheet of paper or a board, list the four elements described in the video that the relief fund will address (Right to Stay, Right to Safe Passage, Welcoming and Belonging, and Right to Return). Invite participants with smartphones or other mobile devices to go to http://www.umcor.com to look for updated news items about Advance#3022144 (Syrian relief) that they can report to the group.

Acknowledge with the group that at this point in the Advent season, most people are well on their way to completing their Christmas shopping, so it may not be feasible to ask people to consider contributing half of what they would spend to the project this Christmas. Discuss the following:

- What needs to be discussed with my family or friends about how we might make a gift to this project or another project that has meaning for us?
- Is there a Christmas gathering we usually have or event we usually spend money on that we might forego or scale back this year in order to make a sacrificial gift to this offering?
- How else might we participate in aiding those who are refugees this Christmas? Are refugees being resettled in our community? If so, how might we contribute to the resettlement process?

Encourage group members to consider how they might participate in meaningful ways in addressing this issue. If your congregation is not already planning to participate in this initiative and your pastor and the mission committee are in agreement, plan to take an offering for Syrian refugees in the last session.

Explore Down-to-Earth Visions

Invite the group to brainstorm a list of crises, troubling issues, or systemic problems in need of action to be taken by Christians, in line with what the group discerns to be God's plan. List these on a board or a large sheet of paper. With a show of hands, determine three or four of these issues to discuss, and invite each participant to self-select one. Form smaller groups of participants who selected the same issue, and give each of these smaller groups the large sheet of blank paper you prepared, as well as markers. Invite the groups to discuss their issue or problem, first determining what their dream would be for those impacted by the problem, and then expressing their vision for how to respond.

After allowing a few minutes for groups to work, ask each group to report to the total group.

Encourage participants to consider this a small first step, recording in their journals some of the steps their group generated for making their vision real. Invite them to include these ideas in their time of prayer, opening themselves to the guidance of the Holy Spirit about how they might act.

Identify Towel Carriers

Review with the group the actions of Dorothy Stang and the Garrett family in emulating the God of the towel. Point out that while these people made exemplary sacrifices, many ordinary Christians also seek to set aside their own privileges in order to live sacrificial, down-to-earth lifestyles.

Distribute paper towels (or copy paper to represent towels) and fine-lined markers to each participant. Invite them to reflect on those people they know and with whom they interact who are "carrying the towel," serving God's kingdom in ways both large and small. Ask them to print the name of one such person on the towel.

After allowing a minute or two for them to reflect and print a name on a towel, ask participants to name the person they identified as a towel carrier, telling what acts of service that person does. Discuss together:

- What actions and qualities of the people we identified demonstrate that they are "towel carriers"?
- What risks has this person taken, or what sacrifices has he or she made, in order to serve God?
- In what ways do these towel carriers serve as an example to us?

Encourage group members to reflect on how they might take actions or alter attitudes in ways that would enable them to grow in sacrificial service. You may want to display the "towels" as a visual reminder for participants.

Wrapping Up

Recall with the group the question they reflected on earlier in the session for writing in their journals:

- Where in my own faith life do I feel called to embrace a lifestyle of sacrificial love?

Encourage them to continue to reflect on this question, perhaps making it a part of their prayer time and meditation during the coming week. Also ask that they read book Chapter 4 and the epilogue prior to the next session.

Closing Activity

Ask:

- What do you think is the greatest act of service a Christian might perform?

Point out the answer given in book Chapter 3 by Mike Slaughter, in the form of the story about how his friend Steve invited him to attend a youth group meeting, an invitation to which Mike Slaughter attributes his own transformation. Encourage participants to invite a friend, work colleague, or acquaintance to a group session or to one of your congregation's Advent events. Then ask them to reflect in silence on the following:

- What does my lifestyle communicate to others about the transforming love of Jesus Christ?
- In what ways do my preparations during Advent communicate sacrificial love to other people who do not have a connection to the church? What do the preparations reveal about my priorities? my commitments?

As group members consider how to extend an invitation to others, encourage them to think about how their actions communicate their Christian faith as effectively as their words.

Closing Prayer

Pray the following prayer, or a prayer of your choosing:

Come, Lord Jesus. Shine the light of discernment on what our lives show others about your radical call. Transform the way we live to more clearly reflect your sacrificial love. For we pray in your holy name. Amen.

4.

Down to Earth Obedience

Planning the Session

Session Goals

As a result of conversations and activities connected with this session, group members should begin to:

- examine how obedience can be redefined as saying a big "yes" to God;
- explore our identity as those who are called together to be followers of Christ;
- embrace what it means to be part of a down-to-earth people, living Jesus' down-to-earth obedience.

Biblical Foundation

Therefore, my dear friends, as you have always obeyed—not only in my presence, but now much more in my absence—continue to work out your salvation with fear and trembling, for it is God who works in you to will and to act in order to fulfill his good purpose. (Philippians 2:12-13)

Special Preparation

- Again set up a simple Advent wreath, with four purple candles, or simply place four candles in a circle. You'll be lighting all four candles with the opening prayer, since this is the final week of Advent and the final group meeting to discuss *Down to Earth*.

- In this chapter, Rachel Billups again uses marriage as an example of a relationship whose dynamics are a metaphor for saying yes. Remember that in most groups, there may be people who have experienced failed marriages, as well as those who have never married, whether by choice or by circumstance. Be sensitive to those persons, and allow room to discuss other relational metaphors besides marriage.

- If you decide to do one or more of the optional activities, check to see what preparation is needed. For the optional activity on putting yourself in Joseph's and Mary's shoes, print the open-ended statements on a large sheet of paper or a board.

- For the optional activity on memory flags, you will need copy paper and colored markers or crayons, a length of cord or string, and tape. Check to see where you may hang the completed flags.

- For the optional activity using the old hymn "Trust and Obey," download the lyrics from the Internet or plan to show one of several YouTube videos of the hymn. You will also need large sheets of paper and markers for the smaller groups.
- For the wrap-up of the study, fold cardstock or stiff paper to make four table tents, and print one of the following on each one: Down-to-Earth Love, Down-to-Earth Humility, Down-to-Earth Lifestyle, Down-to-Earth Obedience. Place one tent in front of each of the four Advent candles.
- For the closing activity, cut stars from construction paper or cardstock, one for each participant. Have pens available.

Getting Started

Opening Activity

Greet participants as they arrive. When most are present, ask them to gather together.

Remind them of the question they were invited to reflect on and pray about in the past week:

- Where in my own faith life do I feel called to embrace a lifestyle of sacrificial love?

Ask volunteers to comment on what they may have discerned about sacrificial love during their times of prayer and reflection.

Call the group's attention to what the writer of this chapter, Rachel Billups, has to say under the heading "Redefining Obedience." Rachel notes that the word *obedience* transported her back to negative experiences during her childhood. For her, obedience was the avoidance of punishment, which she managed by practicing just enough obedience to her parents' rules to avoid getting in too much trouble. Ask participants to call out, popcorn style, words or phrases that come to mind when they hear the word *obedience*. Then ask:

- Which of these words or phrases are tied to negative experiences you have had with the word? Which with positive experiences?
- How do you define *obedience* in your faith life? Is it obeying a set of rules, or is it something else? What problems arise if we equate Christianity with adhering to a set of rules?

Explain that in this final session, participants will have the opportunity to explore a more radical understanding of obedience that involves saying a big "yes" to God.

Opening Prayer

Light all four candles on the Advent wreath. Sit in silence for a few moments, then pray the following, or a prayer of your choosing:

Come, Lord Jesus. As the full light of four Advent candles illuminates the way to your coming, shine your light on new understandings of what it means to be obedient to your call. For in your holy name we pray. Amen.

Learning Together

Video and Discussion

Like any good parent, God has rules, but they're not designed to harm; they're meant to protect. In this session, Rachel Billups discusses what it means to be obedient.

- Rachel says that obedience is forged in the middle of the mess. What does that mean to you, and what are some examples from your own life?
- What can we learn about obedience from the story of Mary when she first got pregnant? What can we learn from the story of Joseph's reaction?
- Rachel talks about having to choose from between good and good, or even great and great. Have you had experiences like that? If so, what did you learn?
- Who are some people whose advice you trust in difficult situations? Why do you trust them?

Bible Study and Discussion

Remind the group that throughout this study, the authors have made use of passages from Philippians 2. Invite volunteers to read aloud the previous passages used, Philippians 2:1-2 and 5-8, along with a new passage, Philippians 2:12-13. Discuss:

- In these passages from Philippians, Paul gave Jesus' followers—and us—a path to saying yes to God. What is the beginning point for "yes"?
- What are some events from God's salvation history, our collective past as Christians, that remind us of who God is?
- After remembering, what is the next step Rachel Billups suggests we must take along the path to "yes"?

Book Study and Discussion

Mary: An Example of the Big Yes

Ask someone to read aloud Luke 1:26-38. Invite others to summarize briefly what Rachel Billups has to say about the circumstances of first-century Palestine in which Mary was living. Also invite a volunteer to review what the group explored in the past session about marriage and betrothal practices. Ask the group to name similarities between Mary's life and the lives of adolescents today. Discuss:

- Where do you see direct parallels? Where are similar kinds of stressors, if not exactly the same?

On a large sheet of paper or a board, print the title "Good News???" Ask group members to name instances of news one might receive that would be far from welcome—those examples Rachel names and others from participants' own lives or the lives of friends and relatives.

Ask the group to look again at the passage from Luke. Discuss:

- What was Mary's response to the question the angel posed?
- In your opinion, did Mary have a choice about obeying God's call or not? Why or why not?
- Rachel states that obedience is much more than simply wishing our circumstances would change. What does she mean, and how do you respond? Is obedience mainly passive, or does it involve intentional action?

Trust and Gratitude

Recall with group members Rachel's statement that, after remembering, trust is the next step to saying yes to God. Discuss some of the following:

- Marriage is one relational situation that involves saying yes. What others can you name? Where have you experienced difficulty in relationships that made it difficult to trust?

- Rachel observes that an attitude of gratitude is called for in all situations—the good, the bad, and the in-between. Do you agree? Why or why not? Do you think feeling gratitude regardless of the situation is a matter of choice?
- When we say thank you, we open up space in our hearts, minds, and souls for God to do new work in us. How does this process work? When, if ever, have you experienced it in your faith life? When have you felt blocked from experiencing gratitude, and what stood in the way?

Ask someone to read aloud Mary's famous song of praise, called the Magnificat, which is found in Luke 1:46-55. Then ask participants to listen as you read from book Chapter 4 the last two paragraphs under the heading "The Path to Obedience" (beginning with "Pause for a moment"). Invite participants to reflect on the questions posed and to respond briefly in their journals. If they are not ready to write responses to the questions, suggest that they copy the two paragraphs in their journals instead and then plan to read and reflect on them in the coming week.

More Activities (Optional)

Put Yourself in Joseph's and Mary's Shoes

Remind the group that in these final two sessions, we learned that Joseph and Mary received news that had to be unwelcome, or at least unsettling. Ask all the men in your group to revisit the account of Joseph's dream in Matthew 1:18-25 and the women to read again the account of Mary's visit from the angel in Luke 2:26-28. Invite both men and women to consider the following questions:

- When I received this news, I was _____ because_____.

- I was deeply worried about what _____ would think and do.
- To be obedient to what God was asking of me, I needed to _____ .

After allowing time for group members to read and reflect on the open-ended statements, invite volunteers to give their responses. Then ask:

- After receiving this news separately from the angels, what might the conversation between Mary and Joseph have been like?

Invite one man and one woman to roleplay that conversation. Then discuss:

- What was involved for Mary and for Joseph in saying yes to God? What did they need to remember? In what or whom did they need to trust?

Create Memory Flags

As people of faith, we need regular reminders of both our collective past—God's salvation history—and our own personal pasts. Invite participants to create memory flags, using this process:

- Ask the group to brainstorm events they can remember from the Old Testament that are part of God's salvation history, such as the Exodus. List these events on a large sheet of paper or a board.
- Distribute copy paper and colored markers or crayons. Ask each person to choose one Old Testament event from the list and use words, phrases, or drawings to illustrate it.
- Then ask participants, on a separate sheet of paper, to use words, phrases, or drawings to illustrate an important

event from their own personal history—an event in which they experienced God's grace and presence. This is their "memory flag."

- Tape completed memory flags to a length of string or cord, and display where others can be reminded of our history as people of faith. If the weather allows, you may want to string the flags outdoors, where the wind can serve as a metaphor for God's Spirit moving through our past and present and as a promise of God's acts of mercy in the future.

Create Additional Lyrics for a Hymn

Invite the group to read silently the lyrics you prepared to the old hymn "Trust and Obey," or show a YouTube video of the hymn. Invite participants to reflect on the meaning of each stanza. Ask:

- What do the words communicate to you about trust and obedience?

Invite participants to review the information in the chapter under the heading "The Path to Obedience." Discuss:

- After reading in Chapter 4 about trust and obedience, do you think there are any ideas missing in what the hymn has to say? Are there understandings about trust and obedience that could be developed further?

Form smaller groups of three or four, depending on the size of your group, and invite each group to create a new stanza for the hymn that expresses something different about trust and obedience. Explain that it's not necessary for the stanza to rhyme. Since it will be helpful for the new stanzas to fit the meter of the hymn, go over the meter of the stanzas (six syllables for the first line, nine for the second, then two lines that repeat the pattern of six and nine syllables). Ask each group to print their completed stanza on a large sheet of paper. After allowing time for groups to work, ask each to report, explaining what they were trying to express and then reading their stanza.

If time allows, add the new stanzas to the hymn and sing or recite it together.

Wrapping Up

Remind the group that in this study, they have been exploring aspects of our true identity as followers of Christ. The name of the study, "Down to Earth," is a play on words that connects Jesus' incarnation—his coming down to earth— with what it means for us to be a down-to-earth people.

Call the group's attention to the table tents you placed in front of the Advent candles. Invite the group to respond in turn to these open-ended statements:

- To live Jesus' down-to-earth love means that we....
- To live Jesus' down-to-earth humility means that we....
- To live Jesus' down-to-earth lifestyle means that we....
- To live Jesus' down-to-earth obedience means that we....

Suggest that in the days leading up to Christmas, participants may want to extend their reflections by rereading the epilogue, "Be Loved. Do Love," seeking a deeper discernment of why Jesus came down to earth and how we live might live more fully as his followers.

Closing Activity

The Apostle Paul wrote that as children of God we can shine like stars. Rachel Billups observes that this does not mean we are extraordinary; rather, it means that God's living spirit shines through us if we are open to that light.

Distribute pens and the cut-out stars, one to a person, that you prepared before the session. Invite participants to think of one action by which they would like their lives to reflect the light of God's spirit to others. It might be through performing some action that shows love, through demonstrating a lifestyle that reflects our calling, through living with humility, or through obeying God's will. Ask participants to print one word on the star that represents that future action, then place the star on the table, grouped with the other stars around the Advent candles. After the closing prayer, participants can retrieve their stars as a reminder of their calling and what they might do about it.

Closing Prayer

Read aloud the words Rachel Billups uses to introduce the closing prayer, then read the prayer itself.

I invite you to pray this prayer with me:

- If you've ever assumed you're too old for anyone to listen to your wisdom...
- If you think you're too young for people to care your dreams...
- If you imagine you have too many problems for anyone to listen to...
- If you've labeled yourself too far gone for God to want you...
- Then let these words wash over you.

Jesus, you came down to earth and moved right into our neighborhood; you became one of us. You did not come so we could pretend to be super-spiritual or superhuman but so your light and love could shine in and through us. Light of the World, shine in the darkest places of our hearts, shine where fear and confusion have left us paralyzed and unable to move forward, shine when we are face-to-face with the question of obedience. Jesus, this Advent and Christmas may we offer to you our simple yes, and may that yes ignite a change in us and in those around us. Give us the grace to shine like stars in the sky so that we will carry your light and love into the world. In your powerful name, Jesus Christ our Lord. Amen.